WHY
CAN'T
IT BE
TENDERNESS

Wisconsin Poetry Series
Ronald Wallace, Series Editor

WHY CAN'T IT BE TENDERNESS

MICHELLE BRITTAN ROSADO

The University of Wisconsin Press

Publication of this book has been made possible, in part, through support from the Brittingham Trust.

The University of Wisconsin Press
1930 Monroe Street, 3rd Floor
Madison, Wisconsin 53711-2059
uwpress.wisc.edu

3 Henrietta Street, Covent Garden
London WC2E 8LU, United Kingdom
eurospanbookstore.com

Printed in the United States of America

This book may be available in a digital edition.

Library of Congress Cataloging-in-Publication Data

Names: Rosado, Michelle Brittan, author.
Title: Why can't it be tenderness / Michelle Brittan Rosado.
Other titles: Wisconsin poetry series.
Description: Madison, Wisconsin : The University of Wisconsin Press, [2018] |
     Series: Wisconsin poetry series | Poems.
Identifiers: LCCN 2018013161 | ISBN 9780299319946 (pbk. : alk. paper)
Subjects: | LCGFT: Poetry.
Classification: LCC PS3618.O7735 W49 2018 | DDC 811/.6—dc23
LC record available at https://lccn.loc.gov/2018013161

for my family

Contents

Acknowledgments

Grateful acknowledgment is made to the editors of the following publications in which these poems or earlier versions, including under other titles, appeared:

Alaska Quarterly Review: "Pastoral with Restless Searchlight"
Grove Review: "Midwinter"
Indiana Review: "Visitations with Unmarried Self"
Los Angeles Review: "The Sky Will Look White"
New Yorker: "Ode to the Double 'L'"
Packinghouse Review: "How to Use Microsoft Paint to Alter a Birth Certificate"
Pilgrimage: "Poem for My Mother"
Poet Lore: "Contemporary Artifacts," "Portrait of His Ex-Lover at a Yoga Studio, Downtown Fresno"
Quarterly West: "Ambivalence"
Sou'wester: "Photograph Taken by My Paternal Grandmother on Her Honeymoon, 1944," "Ritual," "Poem for My Maternal Grandfather"

"Rootless" appeared in the anthology *Time You Let Me In: 25 Poets under 25*, edited by Naomi Shihab Nye (Greenwillow, 2010).

"Lullaby in Which It Becomes Impossible Not to Talk about Race" appeared in the anthology *Only Light Can Do That: 100 Post-Election Poems, Stories, & Essays* (Rattling Wall and PEN Center USA, 2016).

"Poem for My Mother" won the 2010 Academy of American Poets/ Ernesto Trejo Poetry Prize, judged by Philip Levine.

A number of these poems appeared in the chapbook *Theory on Falling into a Reef*, which won the inaugural Rick Campbell Prize (Anhinga Press, 2016).

"On Waking When You're Already Leaving" was set to music by composer Bryan Curt Kostors as part of a longer sequence titled "The Abandoned Hive." It debuted at Boston Court in Pasadena, California, on May 9, 2014.

I am indebted to many individuals for their encouragement, support, generosity, and kindness.

Thank you to David Richards, from whom I first learned to love language and storytelling.

So much gratitude for all my poetry teachers: Bev Conner, Connie Hales, Mark Irwin, Susan McCabe, Carol Muske-Dukes, Hans Ostrom, Tim Skeen, and David St. John.

Special thanks to Cynthia Guardado, Mari L'Esperance, Doug Manuel, Steven Sanchez, and Corinna McClanahan Schroeder—dear friends and trusted readers who helped me shape this manuscript into a book.

My thanks also go to Brian Bernards, Janalynn Bliss, Sara Borjas, Marcus Chinn, Steven Church, Alex Espinoza, Juan Luis Guzmán, Bob Hass, Nancy Hernandez, Lee Herrick, Gabe Ibarra, Miguel Jiménez, Teri Liebel and Rudy Torres, all the Lunas, Simone Muench, Kay Murphy, Laura Musselman-Dakin, Samina Najmi, Viet Thanh Nguyen, Sharon Olds, Claudia Rankine, KS, Arthur Sze, James Tyner, Dagmar Van Engen, and Andre Yang.

Thank you to the Community of Writers at Squaw Valley, the Napa Valley Writing Conference, and the Vermont Studio Center for time and space to write. Thank you likewise to the University of Southern California—especially the Graduate School, English department, and the Creative Writing & Literature program—for ongoing support through grants and fellowships that made the completion of this collection possible. And to the community of poets and writers at California State University, Fresno and the Central Valley, thank you for giving me and this book a place to grow.

Endless thanks to Aimee Nezhukumatathil, for believing in this work and whose own poetry has been a guiding light. Many thanks as well to Rachel Eliza Griffiths, Naomi Shihab Nye, and again David St. John for your thoughtful words and generous spirits. I am so appreciative of the hard work of Ron Wallace and Dennis Lloyd at the University of Wisconsin Press, as well as the rest of the team who helped make this book a reality, including Jennifer Conn, Sheila Leary, Adam Mehring, Sheila McMahon, and Amber Rose.

For love and patience over the years, thank you to my parents, John and Magdalene Brittan; parents-in-law, Eva Moreno and Mariano Rosado; and extended family in both hemispheres, and all who have gone before.

And to Mario and Adrian, my whole heart.

WHY
CAN'T
IT BE
TENDERNESS

ODE TO THE DOUBLE "L"

after Aracelis Girmay

Twin shorelines
at the end
of my name, traffickers
of white space,
you could last on the tongue
forever, lolling, longing,
an endless drawing out
of the little stream
between you.
Fill my life.
I drink from the narrowest
canal, flowing between
two countries
that, half of the time,
claim me. Double "l,"
bring me back
to the in-between
where my breath
has always lived,
without containment,
like two legs pointing
toward the ocean, or these arms
reaching into sky. From birth
you have doubled
my grief and my wonder,
shown me
the parallel
which can never touch—

the way I run
alongside my love
without entering
his true mind. Rivulet
of secrets, slim
as a eucalyptus leaf,
airplane runway
of the heart. Double "l,"
let my days
always move
in two directions.
Build me a channel
into which I can pour
this voice.

WESTERN HISTORY

Sutter, California

Rusted horseshoes

    on a rope above the porch:

clumsy wind chime

    when the air is strong enough.

Arrowheads can be found

    in the yard; and yet,

over a shoulder, lost

    again. Beneath the dirt,

one cement step,

    then another, then

the underground cellar.

    From the wooden beams,

meat hooks

    hang in the dark,

question marks

    for a century

and a half. The answer

    is in the houndstooth

pattern of the brick

    floor. The way out

is the same way I came in.

PASTORAL WITH RESTLESS SEARCHLIGHT

Vacaville, California

I was raised with the ocean
        over my right shoulder
and the jagged mountains filling

        my left hand with teeth, while overhead
the military jets drew their temporary scars.
        In this valley I rocked myself like a marble

at the bottom of a bowl. Then I gathered
        my skirt of drought, of failing
plants. When I slept, the crop dusters laid down

        their thin quilt, and my life shortened,
though barely. I counted my luck
        among the deer drawn down the hill

by the prison's lights. I wanted to
        be like the dried grass alighting suddenly
on a summer afternoon,

        a fire started by nothing
but sun: a helicopter's oracle, foretelling
        the blackened acre like a hole cut

into fabric behind which always breathes
        the tangible dark. I wanted to
be like that, to swallow fences, to listen

        for the animals crossing over,
the night's highway crowded
        with the footsteps of the anonymous.

HOW TO USE MICROSOFT PAINT TO ALTER A BIRTH CERTIFICATE

Spring 1996

Unfolded from its envelope, it is still white,
crisp; she wonders how long it has been shut
in the dark of the lowest drawer of her mother's
nightstand. But on the glass of the scanner, the half
sheet illuminates in a moving stripe
of light—her name bright from one side
to the other, spelling itself through the page
in reverse. Minutes later, the record appears
in grayscale on the computer screen, and the only
tool she needs is the square that erases. Every swipe
of the cursor points an arrow at her birth
before it disappears: San Francisco, the middle
of the night. For a moment, it is blank, a grid
of possibility, binary code of her life smudged
out. But she can rewrite herself, where and when
she was born, and to whom, change
the names she was given before she could speak.
She prints out the cleared boxes, looks for stray
serifs, the dot of an "i" she's forgotten. But she's caught
everything, undone her mother's arrival here, unburdened
her father, sent their planes backward,
uncrossing them over the Pacific. She sets them down
in their places. All of them can start
over now. She writes in her best cursive,
re-creates a biography with dates and places
so no one will be able to tell how this began.

ONLY CHILD

With the mirror at my navel, it appears I'm walking
on the ceiling, house emptied of beds and chairs, all

reduced to fixtures. Everything above me, caught
in the reflection, becomes my path: the downward

slope of roof, recessed lightbulbs that could shatter
under my feet. I step high through doorframes, lift

my legs over the turning blades of the fan. Once,
I saw the planet itself turn upside down

on a screen in the back of an airplane seat, the map
scrolling east toward the island where my mother was born.

But the mirror is a lesser magic than planes.
I haven't gone anywhere, I am still in my father's country—

my country—though it is reversed, a stretch of plaster
that no one has walked on before. I place my hand

against the wall for balance, a hanging plant shoots
its tendrils toward the sky. When I hold up the mirror

to show my parents, it all slips off the edge of the glass.

AMBIVALENCE

as manacle,
joining this

with that.
It's maniacal,

the balance.
Even my name

is an iamb.
So bail me out

of my veins.
One-drop

or the whole
vial, whatever

is viable.
My navel:

a cable
over the Pacific.

What I became:
my own enclave.

DEMENTIA

The suburban development repeats
    itself: houses in khaki,
        seafoam, sky, sienna. Picture window

then door, door then picture window. Every garage
    a jar's seal on the mind. No one is left
        to pace with a cigarette in front of the foreclosures

and their tall grasses. No one is recognizable
    indoors with the air-conditioning on, each face
        the pallor of satellites calling from unfathomable

distances, with the laugh track louder than a key thrown
    over the fence into the canal running behind our yards
        and from which all of us drink—like horses

at a creek before the people came
    to name the place where things had always survived
        without language or memory.

ACROSS THE STREET FROM FOXBORO ELEMENTARY SCHOOL, AN INMATE ESCAPES CALIFORNIA STATE PRISON SOLANO

During lockdown, we play board games
until the teacher rolls in a TV strapped
to its stand, the news coverage offering a view
from the outside. A camera shot

pans over our playground, basketball hoops
that seem high as watchtowers over the man
in a gray jumpsuit suddenly darting across
the courts. Children of Vacaville,

of cowtown, we run to the classroom windows
for a glimpse. What do we know of the world?
We sleep under a sky painted orange
as sherbet by the bright prison lights.

We make field trips to the jelly bean factory,
study its hall of presidential collages: the licorice
hair of Lincoln, Reagan's face made from peach
and buttered popcorn. But we want to see

the inmate's face, the tattoo under his eye
that meant he'd killed someone: the ink outline
of a teardrop, a deflated tetherball, a bubble
of gum hanging from our mouths.

VANISHING SHIP

sculpture by John Roloff (1989)

On the glass surface, a line

    of sap. How nearly I become

what I touch: a half-submerged

    ship in the earth, crystalline.

Stern to sky, stilled rudder

    underground, horizon as infinite sail

in the vast forest of witness.

    Seen right through, the trees

cloud over; behind me, mouthfuls

    of shadow, splintered sun.

My countenance waxes,

    then wanes, between frost

and steam. Crumbling froth,

    nitrogen-rich, I command all things

to grow around my life.

    Hemmed in, I decide

which roots may break me.

THE ELEMENTS HAVE LEARNED TO SPEAK

Whatever it takes for sand to become glass,
    I want that. To be a shard lifted
from the even silt poured from one hand

to another until it became mine. How anything
    came to me out of the suffering
of my elders, I'll never understand. As a child

in San Francisco, wandering the wharf,
    I could stare into a barrel of oysters
all afternoon. The vendor's sign promised a pearl

in each one, a grain of sand carried in a mouth
    until heavy and beautiful. The tourists pulled them
out of the shallow water, ridged with salt

and algae, split them open in their hands
    in search of something worthwhile to take.
What a waste, my mother would say

or I imagined she would say. We'd keep walking
    past the living, symmetrical in their brokenness,
until the pier ended at the edge of the Pacific,

which was the only thing between us
    and our ancestors, a ripped seam between two
hemispheres, on the end of the land's tongue.

THEORY ON FALLING INTO A REEF

I survived on clamshells, a shallow
hunger. Half my skeleton

appears in the sand; the other
stays mine. Pieces

of a bottle, lone button, jar
without its lid. What washed

away? Most of the letters
in my name. Beside the place

I last woke: a rusting nail,
and not the thing that came apart.

*Newly discovered aerial photographs of Gardner Island—now Nikumaroro,
in the South Pacific—suggest Amelia Earhart may have died there, before its
habitation and the arrival of colonists.*

CUSTOMS

At the airport, after a long journey, a mother
and father divide like a cell—foreign
and domestic—into their respective lines
for citizens and noncitizens. The child
is small enough to run beneath the rope
that skims the top of her skull, splitting
her family into parallel routes
to the same house. The girl passes from line
to line, beneath the gaze of the customs officer.
No one has caught her yet, going back
and forth; she swings like a spider
between two points, building something
nearly invisible. *Go to the other side,*
with your father, says the mother. As tall
as suitcases, boxes at eye level, the girl becomes
a piece of luggage in transit. She has nothing
that can be confiscated, she doesn't even hold
her own passport: the adults slide it across
the appropriate counter for an off-center stamp
on an unmarked page. Already she no longer resembles
the child's photo, iridescent and crosshatched
by the advanced security features covering
her face. Even her name has an expiration date,
when, someday, she is married and will change it.
For now, the child belongs to no one and no country,
everything is impermanent—her loyalties
might shift according to a game she makes
of jumping over the dark tiles in the airport floor.

BETWEEN

half   my life grows quiet
the words   crossed out by
a language   what I do not have
I carry it   like a corpse

or a doll   blinking its Morse code
sometimes   my mother
her mouth   opening and closing
a silence   I cannot translate

other times   my father
speaking static   and English
my twin inheritances   braided rope
whatever manages   to clothe me

today the body   I drag behind me
another self   hair gathering dirt
everywhere I go   this throat and its sounds
a music   without meaning

so tired   I cannot leave
I sit her up   leaning against a tree
tie dandelions   into rings
around all her fingers counting time

POEM FOR MY TWIN

Your name holds half of you: like a hammock,
from which your arm and leg dangle, consumed

by mosquitoes, while the rest of your body
is apparently unharmed. Are you marked

or are you pure? It depends
on the angle of the sun and the arrangement

of the trees, and the position of the watcher
who determines the percentage of your face

smothered in light or lowered in shadow.
You press your own palm to your skull,

which has never changed, except when you sleep—
and the watcher is only another tree,

while your breath makes a net strung between two places
that, together, manage to keep you aloft.

OUR BODIES WERE ONCE THE COLOR OF OUR MASKS

after Double Masked Heads *(1974),*
painting by Susan Rothenberg

Two horses stand in profile,   the one behind just barely ahead

like a shadow cast   one second into the future,

or a self beyond the self. Made   from clay, it is possible

to fake their symmetry, become   collapsible, a partial eclipse.

Each of us is made of two   bodies orbiting, both Castor

and Pollux, and you must give   your mouths all the air

that they want. The outline   of one is inseparable

from the other, stepping   together in shadow

more than light. Fold your ears   against the invisible, learn

to trust the wind, your truest   context. Breathe as if

moving a hand toward a candle   then away, flashing a slow message

across the distance. Bear   to love one finger's width

of anything at a time, then pull   your face over your face

if it means surviving   in plain sight.

THE HOTEL EDEN

Break ice plants like dishes
or whatever comes between

your hands and touching
the earth again, even in another

hemisphere. In Borneo,
it's already night. No matter

the names of seeds locked
in square packets. Cut a cross

section in anything that grows
here: notice how zucchini

seeds order themselves in a ring,
even if lost in the mouths

of a family you've married
into. Make beds from any four

slats of wood you find, wait
whole weeks to remember

what you planted there, new
and curling in the fog. Slice

artichokes at the neck, let stalks
sway empty at your shoulder.

Even the thinnest fingers
of ivy unhook with time, leave

blank fences you'll make
every effort to grow over

with carnations before I am born.

ASKING ABOUT MY FIRST NAME

Though my father says he only liked the sound
    of it, the music box seems to offer a better reason
—a hummingbird moving counterclockwise
    on my seventh birthday—because it plays a song

sharing my name. When I wind the key
    on the back, the tiny studs on a cylinder pick
a metal comb, teeth arranged from longest
    to shortest. As it slows to stillness, I turn

this over, run my fingers across the raised dots
    as if I could read them: *I will say the only words*
I know that you'll understand. I can't grasp
    the French parts, but the minor scale is enough

to tell me the song is sad, the way I listen
    to my mother's voice when she calls
back home in her own language, a tinkling sound
    without meaning to me. Silent on another phone

in a different room, I wait for her to speak
    my name—the one word I recognize—but here
it is foreign, like the wrong note played in a melody
    I know well enough to hear the mistake.

DEBT

The father takes down his careful alignment of heads
and tails—buffalo nickels, liberty dollars, half

pennies—from their balancing place on the beams
in the garage roof. He steadies the ladder between

the cars, lowers the books of coins in the dusted light. Lifting
them from their cardboard circles, he shows the girl

the ridged edge that adds worth to one, the rubbed-off
expression of a woman that subtracts from another.

There are letters for each mint—D for Denver, P
is Philadelphia—all of them places she's never been to,

except S, the city both of them are from. Being a child,
she only wants the coincidence of dates: 1953,

when he was born; 1918, his mother. If he gets a bonus this year,
he'll buy more, maybe a roll of silver dimes, or a better Kennedy

fifty-cent piece. He says that luck must be made, the money he earns
pressed down into smaller denominations, what he's certain

will appreciate, while she collects any coin from any year
as long as it's earlier than the one she was born in, as if that makes it

old, and valuable, as if it tells her what came
before, as if they add up to more than their face values.

POEM FOR MY MOTHER

When I was sixteen I bought my mother a strawberry plant
    with its many thin arms hanging over the side
        of its green bowl, each ending with a little fist of white,

yellow, pink, red. She placed it in the front of our house
    and even now it sends its vines through the earth
        beneath a window that faces the street. Every time I visit,

like today, she shows me what new thing came up
    yards away from where it started: a population that dies,
        appears somewhere else. I didn't tell her it reminded me

of the yard we left in San Francisco, the one she spent
    mornings in when this country was so new to her
        she didn't have her job yet and I was too small to be sent anywhere

but there, beside her in the soil. Instead of this I just passed
    the plant to her without a card, only the plastic spike with a Latin name
        for something too awkward, too vital, to wrap in paper.

ROOTLESS

Like a net   my fingers skim

tap water, cleaning   mung bean

sprouts   the way you showed me.

From my palm   I find the whole

ones, fetal   curvatures with scalps

blossoming   on tiny yellowed skulls.

My nail bisects   the vertebrae

from primordial   tail, roots

cast away   in the sink.

Though I never   learned

the purpose, it's a habit   that reminds me

of a time   you let me in.

MY FATHER'S WORK

Even when we move seventy miles outside
      of San Francisco, my father drives back
on weekdays as if to pick up where I started
      and he did, and his father, and another father

before him. This year makes thirty he's spent,
      developing the film containing other people's
lives, in a drugstore on Ocean Avenue. He unrolls
      the brown ticker tape where everyone appears

reversed, even our own family, those miniatures
      still in their paper sleeves though he presses
the glossy prints into album pages under
      cellophane. You could find heavy books of us

at the bottom of our hallway closet, every moment
      that has passed through his fingers; and beneath
their shelf, the neat stacks of film in strips,
      dark versions you could arrange in any order

or pick the one you like best, like my father did
      in my first year, when I was barely able
to stand, but smiling. In the negative, how bright
      our old house would seem around me,

window casting a shadow over my face.

THE SKY WILL LOOK WHITE

You want to be skiing, like the girls in your class who come back
from winter break with photographs of themselves, puffed inside
their jackets. But you're sitting by a window in the house
of your grandfather. Here, it's the monsoon season and you are

fifteen; already you believe you're an artist, insisting
on only the black-and-white rolls of film your father sometimes gets
for free at his job in a drugstore. You're alone in your mother's village,
choosing to stay behind from a drive into the city, because

shopkeepers tease you for not answering *America*
to a question asked in the language you recognize
but don't understand. You don't know how to be grateful,
so you take pictures—elbows propped on the sill, lens pressed beyond

where a screen would be. In two weeks, your father will develop this
picture: the sky will look white, the jungle canopy
drained of green in a deep slope, telephone wires
like a chairlift up the mountain, the raindrops stilled and soft.

PANTUN

Although my relatives are strangers
I sleep with him on their floors
    in a country I'm only visiting.
    A line of gongs through a window

wake me from sleep on the floor
on the morning of Gawai, the harvest.
    Gongs line up past the window
    without a screen to sift the ringing metal

so I know it is Gawai, the harvest.
At the sill I search for people gathering,
    no screen to sift the ringing metal,
    and expect his face in the distance.

At the sill I search for people gathering,
and because he looks like a tourist,
    expect his face to appear, even distant;
    the thin mattress beside me was empty.

In my life, he became a tourist.
His camera is missing from its case
    The thin mattress beside me, emptied,
    gives up the imprint of his body.

His camera unzipped from its case
records my absence in photographs,
    so I give up the imprint of his body
    like a language I've heard since I was born.

He takes photos without me
while I am down the stairs, barefoot,
    following a language I've heard since I was born,
    stepping through mud toward the road.

I am down the stairs now, barefoot,
in a country I've only visited.
    Stepping through mud toward the road,
    I am a relative who is a stranger.

POEM FOR MY MATERNAL GRANDFATHER

Kuching, Sarawak, Malaysian Borneo

I don't know the words to say *I'm here*
in your kitchen with a bowl of fish
and rice, so I leave it next to the bent spoon

on the table. The wood is worn smooth,
but I have never seen you eat here. Through
the window over a gutter, I watch you

pick this over in your hands, in the doorframe
you built yourself. You stare at the path
that brings you what has been set

aside, already cold. Which house
does your wife live in now? Will she ever
return? You try to remember the last meal you ate

together, what it was that made this
final, the scraps and peelings
someone must have finally thrown away.

By now the dish is clean; you toss the bones
into the grass. In the evenings,
the fluorescent lights uncover who is here

and who is not, while the fan turns side to side.

RITUAL

Daly City, California

You always stand in front of the gas flame

 in my memory, five or six eggs rolling at the bottom

of a silver pot. Each week, while my parents are at work,

 I watch the long, slotted spoon pull these up, drop them

into a ceramic bowl to cool. Back in the carton,

 webs of broken shell mark one half from the raw

others. The mornings at your house are quiet,

 and my grandfather lives with another woman.

You make this look easy—waiting, face above the turning

 water, for something to finish itself, only to begin

again—a routine you refused to give up. I'm older

 now; I know how we still lean into the stove like it's a man

we loved, even after he's gone. And how certainly

 the contents of the refrigerator diminish, down

to the last oval swirling its single yolk. Somehow, I can't

    remember seeing you eat them. It must have been

in secret, the peeling of an egg, a handful of ivory

    as you stare out the window into the yard.

PHOTOGRAPH TAKEN BY MY PATERNAL GRANDMOTHER ON HER HONEYMOON, 1944

I don't want her secrets,
only the color of the dashboard
where she rests her bare foot
as her new husband drives
along the Californian coast—
the state where they married,
and will later divorce. The photo
is black and white, only the suggestion
of a window reflecting on her right
arm. There's nothing to see outside
because it's night, and the next town
is miles away. Still she searches for neon
along the road, and for the man
beside her to belong to her again
and not his own concentration
against the surrounding dark.
Twenty-four years is how long
they'll have together, and how old she is
at this moment. A friend once said,
*It may have taken years to learn
he was the wrong person, but it doesn't take
years to leave.* We both know
she's wrong. She listens now only
to the ocean pulling toward the car.

ELEGY WITHOUT TRANSLATION

When everyone had left the room
    to make a late lunch, you began to speak

words I did not understand. I called out
    to the others for translation, but no one

could hear me over the hysterical plates
    and cutlery. You talked over my voice,

my English like sand slipping under the last
    message you'd give me, a length of clear water

pulling away. I listened though I did not know
    the meaning, searched your face and found

only the blue of your cataracts circling iris,
    an island that I would never visit, widening

then contracting with the changing light.

MY DEAD LIVE IN TWO ROOMS

I stagger my visiting   hours. I shuffle

my blood like a deck   of cards I keep

passing across   the table for someone else

to cut by half.   In the afterlife

there is no international   date line, no

jet lag. Still I crack   the spine

of the phrasebook   where it is written

that my only fluency   is being

an outsider.   I knock on the windowpanes

so they know it's me, cousin   to many

and nobody's sister.   The only time they talk

to each other   is in my head. Somehow

we all speak   the same language.

Or nothing   is ever said, only

the thoughtful pause   after someone

is kind, and there   is no use rushing

into the lonely   hallway of a single voice.

THE DISSOLUTION PAPERWORK ASKS
IF I NEED TO RESTORE MY NAME

No, I've kept it, capitalizing
    my father's, block letters
on every sheet as if
    they were my mother's hand

in labor, braceleted white,
    our new name a tattoo
in dot matrix repeating
    narrower on my own

wrist. But I want the name
    before I was named, and this
time I clip it off: turn back
    to Borneo, padi gone to seed

in the field her father would
    neglect, when she worked
carrying his name, knee deep
    in water almost her own.

LATE SUMMER

Tacoma, Washington

Lying on our stomachs,
anything can look infinite—

these fifty-three acres
of blueberries, or a love

nearing its end. Others
here before us

cleared the branches,
so we eat from our palms

what little is left behind.
I fill my pockets

with the unripe ones,
a handful of green

beads; I still believe
he's a necklace

I could string together.
We run through rows

of blueberries until
we reach the city

fences, and watch
the scattering of the broken

blooms we pinch off,
feed to the wind.

SEA SHANTY FOR THE DIVORCED

A candle gives
the illusion of heat.
Water: movement.
How I planted my feet

and believed in
an onward, an infinite wick
but not enough
tallow, a boulder slick

with algae, painted
clear with salt,
what we'd try climbing
anyway. His fault

and mine. All brine
with longing and kelp,
I was more wave
than wax. Felt

the starfish cut
by stone, then grew
a new, a new,
a new, a new.

THE NUMEROLOGY OF US

I told you about it
over dinner:
that she found him
with her cleaver
in the kitchen, right
hand committed
to removing each
finger of his left
at the knuckle,
how many strides
it took to reach
him counting
losses. You were
numbed by these
stories I brought
back from my job
at the mental
hospital, could only
answer me
with fingertips
drumming
the counter whenever
we had to face
the daily effort
of making a living.
How could we
have known
then to number signs
in the patterned
linoleum, notice
divorce sprinting

through the door-
frame? I can't
remember much
of that first
summer—what we were
eating, or how
we'd end
what we'd started—
just a meal
diminishing
between you and me
like words, like
the tally on the cutting
board.

OLD KNIVES

A friend gives me old knives
    sharpened by a butcher, after
        I've moved out and the marriage

is over. Meanwhile, a funeral home
    director in Tennessee went out
        of business, left his last client

on a gurney staring into the blank
    ceiling. I can empathize with one
        who leaves the worst part

as he finds it. Once, I knew to run
    my hands over pepper spray burns
        with mineral oil first, then rubbing

alcohol. Still, no one will believe
    how careful we were; or, when
        we went down in the basement

looking for the fuse box, how my bare
    foot arched over an insect that turned
        back to what was familiar

and farthest. Everything undoes
    itself eventually: for instance,
        the way the body only takes

seven years to replace itself, cell
    by cell. Those lungs were new, the wrists,
        his knees—I took them while I could.

THE TOWER DISTRICT

While we still live
in the same city,

I catch a glimpse
of you, midstride

on the sidewalk
as I drive past,

a moment long enough
to notice you pause—

and I'm certain now
you also recognize

me, my eyes
in the rearview mirror—

until your face
turns away

and you kneel
in the crowd,

growing smaller
over my shoulder,

looking down
toward the concrete

because something
I can no longer see

has just fallen
from your hands

THIS POEM WANTS TO BE A HOUSE

This poem wants to be a house.
Even that first line believes
it can be a roof for the others.
We are still here, though an eye

moves past us. There is life
in the periphery just as sound
fills a far wall within the plaster's
dark. A sheet of cobweb lifts

like a silent wave without land.
Underneath everything—even
the ocean—is packed earth.
The moment I am discovered

to be a stranger, I also become less
of a stranger. Breath spreads a veil
over my face. Someday I will speak
in the doorframe of forgiveness.

FRESNO LAUNDROMAT WITHOUT
AIR-CONDITIONING IN LATE JULY

No one is here, and you can use

    a whole row of washers without

any guilt. You don't bother

    with a cigarette outside, the effort

of self-destruction no longer worth it,

    because you are beginning

to accept that life is, after all, easy:

    it is a level cup of soap flakes

diffusing in water, a matter

    that solves itself. Even with the rattle

of water carving metal, the janitor

    is so quiet emptying quarters

into the hollow of a cardboard box;

    and when you rest against a machine,

he sweeps a careful radius around your feet.

CONTEMPORARY ARTIFACTS

When the box I lower beside me triggers enough
weight, the seatbelt light blinks *passenger*

passenger passenger on the dashboard. Later,
the beams of the headlights will pass over you
waiting in our driveway, to help bring inside

what belonged to me, when I lived with someone
else. He gave me the partial list over the phone,

his voice as strange to me as the furniture
I saw daily for years, the room foreign
in its new arrangement, shelves leaning

into the wall, couch facing away from the door.
On the floor of his apartment, I picked through

the artifacts that say how it was then: a dress
that no longer fits, books I'd made plans to read
and never did. Meanwhile, he boiled water

on the stove in his kitchen, and we drank tea
after I was done, the objects contained and taped

over. As he walked me to my car, the neighborhood
darkened by increments, the sidewalks like lines
drawn between any two points at night. But now,

you carry this in your arms over the broken
porch step. In our room, this fits beneath the bed.

PORTRAIT OF HIS EX-LOVER AT A YOGA STUDIO, DOWNTOWN FRESNO

The tattoo of a flower on her left shoulder
    enters my vision as we both turn

at the waist toward the window
    beside each other. Outside, the gates

of the factory across the street
    close for the evening, and the lamps

burn at measured distances. Now
    we have an hour of our paired breathing,

the industrial district going dark,
    an occasional train that comes close

then curves away. I watch her
    whole body for clues on where to bend

next—shadow on the brick wall
    larger than both of us—my movements

always a second after hers. I'd rather
    hear her voice, know anything else

besides her neck arched to the raftered
    ceiling when we lie down, edges

of her mat only inches away. Arms
    outspread, we could touch.

INCIDENT BETWEEN TWO EXITS

While the seatbelt unfurls   a lilac bruise

over my chest, ribbons   of smoke

rise from the crushed   hood, taillights

staining them in monochromatic   reds

before releasing   into dusk. The destroyed

horn sounds a single   note announcing

my life's continuation: skinned knees

below the dashboard,   single-seated pew

and the abstract   mosaic suddenly formed

across the wind   -shield, all radio hush

in the cathedral   of my brain. What words

could I mouth   to the drivers tarrying

to witness, what could I   possibly say

from the interior   of a burst bloom

of silver? I was   complete, I counted

my fortune on both sides   of the center divide—

those innumerable   sequins of glass.

WHY CAN'T IT BE TENDERNESS

Follow any road in Fresno and it will narrow
to gravel, the line down the center

disappearing amid the stripes of almond
saplings and grapevines for miles.

If you trace a trajectory long enough, it loses
its name. I left that life years ago

and I've been calcifying on the shore ever since.
Change your idea of brokenness. Today's salt

is mine, and tomorrow's. Look for me
on the horizon. I am as small and endless as sand.

THE SWEETEST EXILE IS THE ONE YOU CHOOSE

Beyond the body. Beyond the car.
Beyond the wire pulled loose

on a fence still waving the flag
of torn things. Beyond the tall grasses

and the shorn hillside. Beyond
the dried-up canal, the empty tent

with the dead fire outside it, the broken
reflector flashing distantly

at the foot of a burned-out barn. Beyond
this valley. Think *ocean*, think

lost continent. Beyond the dead
and their failures: knowledge they took

nowhere. Beyond the point
of anything calling your name. Call

your own name. Beyond the voice
no longer ringing, like a hubcap flung

into stillness. Beyond the bridge
your words make, the heartbeat's

trapeze. Beyond the radio tower
blinking its one red light. Beyond

the emergency call boxes
spaced like old hurts you gather up

for miles. Beyond the ordinary
narrative of being. Beyond

the bird's nest. Beyond the bird's nest
coming apart in the rain.

A NAME MADE OF ASTERISKS

Mine contains one hundred

    and seventeen, each five-armed star
        a shut mouth. Los Angeles,

           you say too much. From the Blue Line
               this morning: a heap of empty bathtubs
           taller than all the buildings in Watts.

        When I imagine his life now,
    the tops of the palm trees

spell something I can no longer read.

MISTAKEN ODE

I have made so many mistakes, lucky
to have been mine—oh how I relive them,
middle-of-the-night looped reels

of them. I call them back to me, I must
not leave any of them out, all the crayons
in the right place, I am working

toward a complete set, my shelves are filled
and alphabetized. I take armfuls with me
for company on road trips, we sing harmony

together the whole way to nowhere, I look
for mistakes hitching on the side of the highway
with tidy bindles of self-loathing, I commit

their stories to memory, I give them all
nicknames: Feeling That Wasn't
Love, Doomed Marriage, Kicked Dent

in a Car Door after a Fight. I take them down
from a cabinet to polish them every Sunday,
I hoard them like animals, I keep photos of them

in my wallet and show strangers in waiting rooms.
My mistakes love me back with a feeling so pure
I get dizzy, how did I get so fortunate, no one

has mistakes like mine, people ask *where did you*
get that and I make up exotic locations
though I suppose my mistakes are as common

as Target-brand napkins, repeating patterns
on the tissue of my brain. My mistakes
are so absorbent I can wipe up a small one

with a bigger one and temporarily forget the small
one, but now my heart is a rag with no bleach left
in it, all the dark water of my mistakes wrung out

in a bucket, I wash my windows with them,
I set them out like jewelry in the evenings
in infinite combinations and they all turn

my wrists green, there is no use pawning them
because I'd buy them all back, I wear them
the next day, and the next and the next.

LOVE AFTER DENTISTRY

With my mouth half-numb against yours,
                the palm on my face might as well touch
anyone's. I can't feel your thumb pulling down
                my bottom lip, index resting

under the chin, even though it's a habit made familiar
                to me now. I have to rely on sight
to know what you're doing, your eyes closed
                against the memory of another woman

for all I know. Beyond us and the wall
                of the room, the grass stretches toward the end
of the yard. I could call up the fingers
                of someone else; I've done it

before. It was a kind of test, the recollection
                of the last man like a layer
over your movements so that, for a second,
                the two of you blurred. And I would

do the work of finding you—the pressure
                of your arm behind my back, your hip
on the inner side of my thigh—just to separate
                your touch from his, and in this way

I could choose you over and over. Maybe
                you've done the same, there may have been times
my body changed under your body, it's possible
                you did not know who I was until I returned

to you as myself, and whatever light

                          the day had left would uncover our faces

to each other. But this time I turn my head, run

                  my tongue over the raw surfaces in my mouth

for the first time, while the fence outside

                        the window arranges itself in parallel

lines. Here are the new spaces, the hard

                    plaster sanded over, my own teeth.

ON WAKING WHEN YOU'RE
ALREADY LEAVING

The slide of the bolt and lock, fingers
snapped at the end of a spell—your body

walking to the car under the inscrutable
graffiti of the stars—invisible garland

of your green bar of soap still
hanging aromatic in the dim hallway

outside the shower—the steam retreating
to the mirror's oval border, my face

appearing after yours in the cleared
center—the tiny light

on the coffee pot burning at the back
of the kitchen, a pinhole in the night's last

darkness—the pan you cooked eggs in,
the filigree of yellow along the edge

in a ring, lifted out whole like a crown.

MIDWINTER

While he is gone, all she can

    stomach are tangerines, the globes

that give December a color. She inserts

    a thumbnail, the peel moistens

cuticle, the fruit rips free from its zest.

    She counts the segments, sometimes

odd in number so the halves come out

    uneven. Bits of rind scale off

like a sunburn and her tongue loosens

    the seeds from under the skin, drops

them into her palm. The curves

    look pitiful: semicircles half-

full or half-gone. Drawing out one

    long bead of pulp at a time,

such small increments she can taste

    the tartness, she wants nothing to replace

the memory of his mouth—not even

    this bit of nourishment, the only flesh

she can bear to touch.

AN ANCHOR IN THE SHAPE OF AN AMPERSAND

"the experiences of exiles are incommunicable"
—Édouard Glissant, *The Poetics of Relation*

and the wave
of your hand passing

over my face,
brief island

of morning,
in which nothing

existed
before, yet the wind

comes &
from some-

where,
the bedroom

window fills
the sheer

curtain with light,
blank

day all bedsheet
horizon, where we turn

like compasses,
toward something

unnamed

VISITATIONS WITH UNMARRIED SELF

You keep coming back: the maiden name
    on grocery store mailers, special offers

from magazines I subscribed to
    in another life. I hardly recognize you—

you don't even know you're a ghost,
    slithering from mouths

and out-of-date medical records,
    pacing waiting rooms invisibly

until I answer for you. You are still
    registered to vote, believing you are part

of the future, where you cast your wishes
    into the great uncounted. You are like the dead

who cannot understand how time moves
    on without them. I tell you this in public

bathroom mirrors while I press
    our faces together. Or you are like a child

following the mother absorbed
    in the list of things she piles into a cart.

Her life is an eclipse moving slowly
    over yours, which you can only watch

swallow the light, your one
    belonging. It's over, it's over, the long illness

of being your own. Everyone gathered to say
    goodbye, in dry-cleaned skirts

and rented suits, confetti clutched
    like ash. Over my shoulder I threw

to you flowers, but already you entered
    me, and I was possessed.

I blanched then, white as a dress.

GLAUCOMA TEST

I adjust for memory, the optometrist says.

   E O T V

I say. Something with three lines, something
   circling nothing, something flattened
by sky, something broken by gravity.

   We talk to each other like this in the dark.
He tilts my head back; my pupils widen
   from left to right. Then I'm alone.

Darkness, blurred, is not much different
   from the usual darkness. In another room,
he tells his assistant the results,

   in a lexicon that joins them together
in mutual understanding. I've been listening
   to the languages of others all my life

and all of it's a music that's not mine.
   How do you say my name in Chinese,
the kids at school said, pulling

   their eyelids back. I imagine my face
would blur: lost precision of my life,
   squinted at. It's a poverty

to have only one language for grief,
    a devastation to have two. At night,
while asleep, my love begins speaking

    sounds that do not take the shape of words
in my first language or in his. In the morning,
    I say, *You were talking in a dream.*

I don't remember, he says, *only you falling*
    asleep first, and the night somehow
passing with both of us inside it.

LULLABY IN WHICH IT BECOMES IMPOSSIBLE NOT TO TALK ABOUT RACE

All night, the rusted water heater
rocks gently on its side,

useless in the dried grass. I imagine

even ideas must sleep sometimes:
race, for instance,

has a recurring dream of a bathroom mirror

in which none of our faces are changed
by history. Meanwhile, most of my waking

life has been spent trying to remember

if the moon is waxing
or waning. At any moment

I can never tell if I'm disappearing

into myself, or at the edge
of something that could alter

the whole sky.

Notes

"Ode to the Double 'L'": With thanks to Aracelis Girmay's "Ode to the Little 'r'" from *Kingdom Animalia*.

"Vanishing Ship": John Roloff's sculpture *Vanishing Ship* is permanently installed at the Djerassi Resident Artists Program in Woodside, California. With thanks to Mari L'Esperance.

"Our Bodies Were Once the Color of Our Masks": Susan Rothenberg's painting *Double Masked Heads* is part of the collection at the Broad museum in Los Angeles, California.

"The Hotel Eden": With thanks to Joseph Cornell's sculpture of the same name. I saw it in a photograph, though it is part of the collection at the National Gallery of Canada in Ottawa, Ontario.

"Asking about My First Name": "Michelle" is featured on the Beatles' *Rubber Soul* album, which was released in 1965.

"Debt": Coinage produced at the San Francisco Mint bears an "S."

"Pantun": The pantoum was adapted from the *pantun*, a Malay poetic form.

"Late Summer": Blueberry Park is free to all visitors, and owned by Metro Parks in Tacoma, Washington. Picking season is from July through September.

"The Tower District": The Tower District is a neighborhood in Fresno, California.

Wisconsin Poetry Series
Ronald Wallace, Series Editor

How the End First Showed (B) • D. M. Aderibigbe
New Jersey (B) • Betsy Andrews
Salt (B) • Renée Ashley
Horizon Note (B) • Robin Behn
About Crows (FP) • Craig Blais
Mrs. Dumpty (FP) • Chana Bloch
The Declarable Future (4L) • Jennifer Boyden
The Mouths of Grazing Things (B) • Jennifer Boyden
Help Is on the Way (4L) • John Brehm
Sea of Faith (B) • John Brehm
Reunion (FP) • Fleda Brown
Brief Landing on the Earth's Surface (B) • Juanita Brunk
Ejo: Poems, Rwanda, 1991–1994 (FP) • Derick Burleson
Jagged with Love (B) • Susanna Childress
Almost Nothing to Be Scared Of (4L) • David Clewell
The Low End of Higher Things • David Clewell
Now We're Getting Somewhere (FP) • David Clewell
Taken Somehow by Surprise (4L) • David Clewell
Borrowed Dress (FP) • Cathy Colman
Places/Everyone (B) • Jim Daniels
Show and Tell • Jim Daniels
Darkroom (B) • Jazzy Danziger
And Her Soul Out of Nothing (B) • Olena Kalytiak Davis
My Favorite Tyrants (B) • Joanne Diaz
Talking to Strangers (B) • Patricia Dobler
The Golden Coin (4L) • Alan Feldman
Immortality (4L) • Alan Feldman

(B) = Winner of the Brittingham Prize in Poetry
(FP) = Winner of the Felix Pollak Prize in Poetry
(4L) = Winner of the Four Lakes Prize in Poetry